SUPER SPORTS STAR
★ STAR
GLEN RICE

Ken Rappoport

Enslow Publishers, Inc.

40 Industrial Road   PO Box 38
Box 398   Aldershot
Berkeley Heights, NJ 07922   Hants GU12 6BP
USA   UK

http://www.enslow.com

Library of Congress Cataloging-in-Publication Data

Rappoport, Ken.
   Super sports star Glen Rice / Ken Rappoport.
      cm. – (Super sports star)
   Includes bibliographical references (p.) and index.
   ISBN 0-7660-1808-3
   1. Rice, Glen—Juvenile literature. 2. Basketball players—United States—Biography—Juvenile literature. [1. Rice, Glen. 2. Basketball players. 3. African Americans—Biography.] I. Title. II. Series.
   GV884.R52 R37 2002
   796.332'092—dc21

                                    2001001917

Printed in the United States of America

10 9 8 7 6 5 4 3 2 1

To Our Readers:
We have done our best to make sure that all Internet addresses in this book were active and appropriate when we went to press. However, the author and publisher have no control over and assume no liability for the material available on those Internet sites or on other Web sites they may link to. Any comments or suggestions can be sent by e-mail to comments@enslow.com or to the address on the back cover.

Photo Credits: Al Messerschmidt/NBA Photos, p. 11; Andrew D. Bernstein/NBA Photos, pp. 31, 37; Barry Gossage/NBA Photos, pp. 19, 21; David Liam Kyle/NBA Photos, p. 39; Fernando Medina/NBA Photos, p. 24; Glenn James/NBA Photos, p. 41; Jon Hayt/NBA Photos, p. 4; Nathaniel S. Butler/NBA Photos, pp. 1, 6, 26; Noren Trotman/NBA Photos, pp. 15, 33, 44; Rocky Widner/NBA Photos, p. 13; Scott Cunningham/NBA Photos, pp. 17, 34; Victor Baldizon/NBA Photos, pp. 9, 29.

Cover Photo: Nathaniel S. Butler/NBA Photos.

4.4

0.5 points

Withdrawn

CONTENTS

Introduction 4

1 A Pressure Situation 6

2 Growing Up in Flint 11

3 Mr. Basketball 17

4 Breaking Out 24

5 Mr. Reliable 29

6 Shooting Star 33

7 Getting Comfortable 37

Career Statistics 43

Where to Write 44

Words to Know 45

Reading About and
Internet Addresses 47

Index 48

Introduction

Glen Rice's shooting talents are amazing. He plays for the Houston Rockets. He is one of the best outside shooters in the National Basketball Association (NBA). When he is on his game, few are better at making 3-point shots. Rice also has a classic jump shot closer to the basket. And he is one of the league's best foul shooters. But he is more than that. Some people think of him as two players in one.

At six feet eight inches tall, Rice is a big guard who can run the offense. He is usually taller than the players that guard him. He can shoot, dribble, and pass.

Glen Rice can also play the forward position. He is often quicker than the players who guard him. He can shoot from outside and inside. He can drive to the basket. He can rebound.

Glen Rice is usually among the top players in the NBA year after year. He is a three-time all-star and an NBA champion.

A Pressure Situation

The pressure was on Glen Rice. In 1989, after college he came to the NBA to play for the Miami Heat. He was expected to be their star player. Now it was his second season in the NBA, and he was still having trouble fitting in.

Where was the great shooter that led Michigan to the national title? He had been one of the top college players in the country.

The Heat were just in their second year in the NBA. They had finished last in scoring in the NBA the season before. They were counting on Rice's scoring talents. But Glen Rice had come to the team overweight and out of shape. His teammates teased him. They called him "Puffed Rice."

He worked hard over the summer after his first year in the NBA. He was in better shape in his second season. Teammates stopped teasing him. He had practiced his dribbling and driving to the basket. He also practiced his defense. "I knew that I could develop into a star player if

I put in the extra time and effort that it takes," he said.

But so far, the hard work had still not paid off. Late in his second season, his scoring average was lower than expected. He had done much better in high school and college. At Miami, Rice was having trouble making the three-point shots. In the NBA, the three-point line is twenty-three feet nine inches away from the basket. That is four feet further away than in college basketball. Rice was having a hard time getting used to the difference.

Had the Heat made a mistake by making Rice their No. 1 pick in the college draft? Rice even started to wonder. Early in February 1991, the Heat went to Orlando for a game against the Magic. In the second quarter the Heat trailed, 31–25. Rice was still struggling. He had not yet scored a point.

Suddenly, with 9:28 remaining in the half, Rice connected on a three-pointer. Twenty-four seconds later, he scored another. The Magic

After college, Glen Rice went to play for the Miami Heat in the NBA.

could not stop Rice, and Rice could not miss. Within ten minutes, he had scored 23 points! That was more than many players scored in an entire game. The Heat led, 54–53, at halftime. Rice finished with 37 points. That was the most points he had scored since joining the NBA.

Rice's great shooting did not result in a win for the Heat. But the team had a reason to feel good. Glen Rice had finally started shooting the ball well in the NBA.

Growing Up in Flint

It was nighttime in Flint, Michigan. Glen Rice would not come in from the dark. He had been playing basketball for most of the afternoon with his brother Kevin. There were no lights on the court. But they still played after dark. The only light came from a street lamp more than one hundred feet away.

Somehow, twelve-year-old Glen found the rim with his jump shot. He kept making his shots from twenty, twenty-five feet away. Swoosh . . . Swoosh . . . Swoosh . . . One shot after another, the ball dropped through the basket. Today, Rice is known as one of the best shooters in the NBA. Those nights shooting baskets in the dark helped. "We couldn't see the rim at all," Rice said. "We could barely make out the net. It was hard at first. That's how I developed my shooting eye."

Before Glen Rice could become a well-known basketball star, he had to overcome his fears. As a child, he was tall for his age. But he was also very skinny. He played against the bigger, rougher neighborhood kids and got pushed around a lot. After a while, he stopped playing with them. He was afraid he might get hurt. He chose to play with his younger brothers, Kevin and Daron, or by himself. "I just enjoyed shooting," he said.

Glen Rice was born on May 28, 1967, to

As a child, Glen Rice developed his shot playing basketball at night on the neighborhood court.

Thomas and Ernestine Rice. The family lived in Jacksonville, Arkansas, until Glen's mother moved the family to Flint, Michigan. She raised her four children on her own. Glen had a sister, Veronica Michelle, and two brothers, Kevin and Daron.

The family was poor. "I remember being frustrated the whole ninth grade because I only had three pairs of pants," Glen said. "People talked about that. My brothers were the same size so they could wear each other's clothes. But I couldn't."

As a boy, Glen was a "loner." He enjoyed being by himself. One of his favorite things was playing video games. "I'd go to the video arcades when I'd get my hands on some change," he said. "And I'd always pretend I was in the box, fighting the dragons and all the bad guys."

Finally, Glen got up enough courage to join the junior high school basketball team. He would show everyone he could play.

When he was young, Glen Rice enjoyed being by himself. That changed when he hit the basketball court.

Two years later, Glen led Flint Northwestern High School to a state championship. Then he did it again. In his last year of high school, Rice averaged about 25 points a game. He won the title of "Mr. Basketball" in Michigan. It is given every year to the best high school senior in the state.

Glen was beginning to get more confidence. But he never dreamed he would play for a big-time college basketball team. After high school, he was on his way to the University of Michigan. What did his future hold?

Mr. Basketball

Glen Rice met Bill Frieder, the coach for the University of Michigan, when Frieder was a high school coach in Flint. The coach liked what he saw when he watched Glen Rice play in high school. So, he gave Glen Rice a scholarship (money to pay for college) to the University of Michigan.

The University of Michigan team had many good players. Rice was not needed right away, but he was noticed in practice.

Glen Rice had friends among the players. He loved the school, and it was close to home. But one thing worried him. Was he big and tough enough to stand up to the other players he would play against? The players in this league were very physical. But Rice learned how to be tough while facing his teammates in practice. "I started to get stronger," he said.

Rice was used mostly as a replacement player for the first two years of college. He still led the Big Ten in rebounding in his second year. The season ended on an unhappy note

Glen Rice became a stronger basketball player during college.

for the team, though. The Wolverines were unable to reach their goal of winning the NCAA title.

"The younger guys on the team talked about it a lot," Rice said. "We knew when we got to be juniors and seniors we weren't going to let that happen."

In his third year, Glen Rice led the league in scoring. Michigan still did not win the national title, though. Some people said that maybe Rice would leave school early to join the NBA. But Glen Rice was staying. He wanted to keep his promise to help the Wolverines win a championship.

In Glen's last year in college, the team was on its way. Rice won his second straight Big Ten scoring title. He was great in the regular season. In the 1989 NCAA playoffs, he was even better. He came close to breaking the all-time playoff scoring record set by Princeton's Bill Bradley in 1965. "This is the best stretch I've ever had," Rice said.

Winning the Championship game in his last year at the University of Michigan was just the beginning of Rice's basketball career.

Coach Frieder was no longer with the team. Assistant Coach Steve Fisher was now the head coach. But, the Wolverines still played well. They beat all five teams they faced in the playoffs. Now they were in the finals against the Seton Hall Pirates. If they won this game, they would win the championship.

The Wolverines built a 12-point lead. Then they lost it. The game ended in a tie. Overtime was needed to decide a winner. The teams kept the score close in overtime. With 12 seconds left, Seton Hall had a 79–78 lead. The Pirates held the ball and had a chance to win.

But Rice forced two missed shots by the Pirates' John Morton. After the second shot, Rice grabbed the rebound. It was his eleventh rebound in the game. He passed to his teammate Rumeal Robinson, who was racing down the court. Robinson

★ ★ **UP CLOSE**
★

Glen Rice likes to play video games. He says, "I am crazy about video games. Basketball and football are my favorites."

was fouled going up for the shot. He sank two free throws and Michigan won, 80–79. The Wolverines were champions!

Glen Rice had scored 31 points. He finished with 184 points for the tournament. But he had showed every college basketball fan he was more than just a scorer. Now he wanted to show the NBA what he could do.

CHAPTER 4

Breaking Out

It was the spring in 1992 and Miami had been hit by a Heat wave. It had nothing to do with the weather. It was instead the great play of the NBA's Miami Heat.

After four seasons in the NBA, the Heat finally had a chance to make the playoffs. And Glen Rice was leading the way. It had taken Rice nearly two years to play well in the NBA. Now, game after game, he was lighting up scoreboards around the league.

Basketball fans in Miami had been waiting for Rice to break out. So had the Miami Heat. The Heat had made Glen Rice their first pick in the 1989 NBA draft. He was supposed to be their top player.

In his third year as a pro, Rice finally looked like a real pro. He had become the most improved player in the league. He had worked hard in the off-season to lose weight. And he had worked hard on his game. His dribbling, passing, and defense all improved.

Glen Rice was named the league's player of

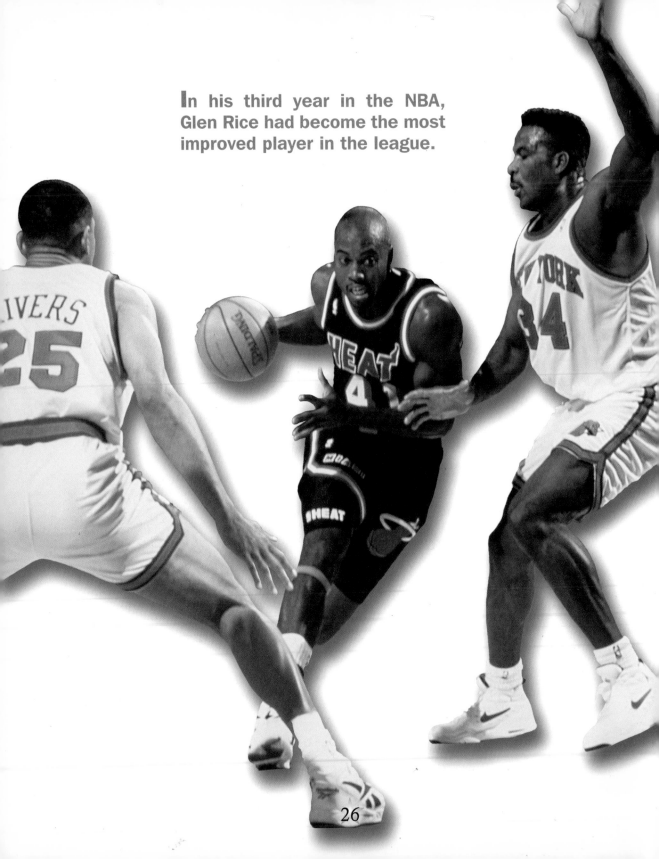

In his third year in the NBA, Glen Rice had become the most improved player in the league.

the month for April. He averaged about 26 points in nine games. It was a good time for him to be playing so well. The Heat were trying to earn a spot in the playoffs.

Late in the 1991–92 season, the Heat faced the Orlando Magic. It was a game the Heat had to win to stay in the playoffs. The game went back and forth. Glen Rice and Orlando's Nick Anderson matched almost shot for shot. When Rice scored his forty-sixth point, he set a team record. Three seasons later, also against Orlando, Rice would set a new team scoring record with 56 points. But for now, he turned his attention to rebounding to help his team. With five seconds left, he grabbed the ball out of the air to help Miami keep the lead. Two free throws by the Heat wrapped up a 105–101 victory. "I went out tonight really wanting to take control of the game," Rice said.

By the end of the season, the Heat had reached the playoffs. No one expected the Heat to win the NBA championship. They were a young team with not much playoff experience. But the Chicago Bulls found out they were not going to be easy to beat. Michael Jordan and the Bulls worked hard to finally knock Miami out of the playoffs.

"We showed people what the Heat is going to be like in the future," Rice said. Glen Rice had certainly shown that he could be a team leader and a superstar.

Mr. Reliable

Glen Rice scored a record-setting 56 points to help the Miami Heat beat the Orlando Magic, 123–117, in a game during the 1994–95 season.

During the season, 30-point games were common for the Miami Heat's star shooter. But a 56-point game put Rice in the same category as Michael Jordan. The Chicago Bulls' star had scored 55 points earlier in the season.

It had been quite a year for Glen Rice. At the All-Star Game, he won the Long Distance Shootout. He stood beyond the three-point line and put shot after shot through the net.

For the Heat, Glen Rice was the only Miami player to play in all 82 games that season. He scored 1,831 points, the most of his six-year NBA career.

The Heat missed the playoffs that year, but Rice had become a superstar. He finished the season with a 22.3 average. He was one of the top ten scorers in the NBA.

Glen Rice shows off his classic shooting style as his defenders look on.

Then one day, his world was turned upside down. On November 3, 1995, he was on his way to practice when his phone rang. It was Miami's coach, Pat Riley. Rice had been traded to the Charlotte Hornets.

"I just went back inside, sat down on my living room floor and cried," Rice said.

As Glen Rice headed for Charlotte, he was unsure what the future held.

Shooting Star

It was not just another NBA All-Star Game. Basketball's all-time greatest players were all there for the "NBA at 50" event. It was 1997 and it was the league's fiftieth birthday. Fifty of the greatest NBA players in history were honored at the Gund Arena in Cleveland. "I was watching the legends at halftime and I was just in awe," said Glen Rice, who was a reserve for the game.

Rice was playing in his second straight All-Star Game since his trade to Charlotte. He had never made the All-Star team in his six years in Miami. Now he was making it a habit.

During the 1996–97 season, Rice looked like an all-star.

During the 1996-97 season, Rice truly looked like an all-star. He drove to the basket, grabbed rebounds, and scrambled after loose balls. He had also improved his defensive play, and the Hornets improved along with him.

Rice had an extra push to become a "complete player." It came from his future wife, Cristy Fernandez. They always talked about basketball. She would tell Glen what he could do to play his best. At first, he did not listen. Then during one game during the 1995-96 season, Rice was sitting on the bench. He heard a voice behind him. "She was chewing on me. *On the bench*!" Rice's feelings were hurt. But he soon took Cristy's advice.

He started the 1996–97 season with a new way of thinking. He was suddenly one of the hottest players in the league. Before the All-Star Game, he had been on the best scoring streak of his eight-year pro career.

★★★ **UP CLOSE**

During the holidays, Glen Rice visits children in hospitals.

In the first half of the All-Star Game, he did not look like the same Glen Rice. He took seven shots. He made only one for two points. He had not lost his confidence, though. "No matter how many shots I'm missing, I really try to stay focused," he said. The NBA greats were honored at halftime. After that, Rice started to look like his old self.

In the third quarter, he hit a three-point shot. Then he hit another, and still another. Rice made 8 of 11 baskets from all over the court in the third period. By the end of the game, he had scored 24 points in the second half. He broke the record of Hall of Famer Wilt Chamberlain. Glen Rice was voted the game's Most Valuable Player and the East won, 132–120. He had picked a special moment to win MVP. "It was great to do it in front of all these guys," he said of the NBA greats.

Getting Comfortable

In 1999, Glen Rice was traded again. This time he went to the Los Angeles Lakers. Rice usually controlled the ball and did most of the shooting for his team. He would be doing different things for the Lakers.

The Lakers already had two of the league's top players, Shaquille O'Neal and Kobe Bryant. They needed a good outside shooter to complete the picture. They hoped Glen Rice would be that man.

Rice got off to a good start when he scored 21 points against Golden State. It was his first game for the Lakers. But as the season went on, Rice was not happy. He was shooting less. His scoring average dropped. He was not enjoying himself. "I'd be lying if I told you it wasn't frustrating," Rice said. The brightest moment of the year for Rice was the birth of a daughter, Brianna.

The Lakers did not win the championship in 1999. That only made Rice more unhappy. The Lakers looked forward to another chance in

The Lakers hoped that Glen Rice would be the outside shooter they needed.

the 1999–2000 season. Glen Rice was ready to help his team win it all. But Rice had a hard time keeping his mind on basketball. There were rumors he would be traded. He was relieved when it did not happen.

On his thirty-third birthday, Rice had a big night. He scored 21 points and had 7 rebounds. And the Lakers won their playoff game against the Portland Trail Blazers. The Lakers continued to win. Their next stop was the finals against the Indiana Pacers. After five games, the Lakers held a 3–2 lead. With one more win, the title would be theirs.

In Game 6, the Lakers were holding a shaky 110–109 lead with about a minute left in the game. Rice drove down the lane toward the basket. He was fouled. He made both shots to give the Lakers a three-point lead. Rice's free throws were the winning points. The Lakers won the title, 116–111. As expected, O'Neal and Bryant led the way for the Lakers. But Rice

In 2000, Glen Rice was traded to the New York Knicks.

had also played well. He had scored 16 points and played well on defense.

During the summer, Glen Rice was unsure of his future. There was only one thing for sure. He did not want to return to the Lakers. He got his wish. The Lakers traded him to the New York Knicks. It was a twelve-player, four-team deal. Rice had won a title in Los Angeles. Now he was ready to help the Knicks do the same.

The 2000–2001 season brought a playoff appearance for Glen Rice and the Knicks. Unfortunately, they did not get past the Toronto Raptors in the first round.

In the 2001–2002 season, Rice found himself with a new team. The Knicks had traded him to the Houston Rockets. This made Rice happy. In New York, he had a hard time fitting in with the Knicks. A hurt leg added to his problems.

Now in Houston, Glen Rice was ready to return to the all-star form that had made him one of the top shooters in the NBA.

CAREER STATISTICS

				NBA					
Team	Year	GP	FG%	Reb.	Ast.	Stl.	Blk.	Pts.	Avg.
Miami	1989–90	77	.439	352	138	67	27	1,048	13.6
Miami	1990–91	77	.461	381	189	101	26	1,342	17.4
Miami	1991–92	79	.469	394	184	90	35	1,765	22.3
Miami	1992–93	82	.440	424	180	92	25	1,554	19.0
Miami	1993–94	81	.467	434	184	110	32	1,708	21.1
Miami	1994–95	82	.475	378	192	112	14	1,831	22.3
Charlotte	1995–96	79	.471	378	232	91	19	1,710	21.6
Charlotte	1996–97	79	.477	318	160	72	26	2,115	26.8
Charlotte	1997–98	82	.457	353	182	77	22	1,826	22.3
Los Angeles	1998–99	27	.432	99	71	17	6	472	17.5
Los Angeles	1999–2000	80	.430	327	176	47	12	1,272	15.9
New York	2000–01	75	.440	307	89	41	13	899	12.0
Totals		900	.454	4,145	1,977	917	257	17,542	19.3

GP—Games Played   Ast.—Assists   Pts.—Points per Game
FG%—Field Goal Percentage   Stl.—Steals   Avg.—Average points per Game
Reb.—Rebounds   Blk.—Blocked Shots

Where to Write to Glen Rice

Mr. Glen Rice
c/o the Houston Rockets
2 Greenway Plaza, Suite 400
Houston, TX 77046

WORDS TO KNOW

All-Star Game—A game held in mid-season, matching the top players in the Eastern Division against the best of the Western Division.

Big Ten—A group of college teams that play against each other.

center—The team's biggest player who does most of the rebounding and shot blocking.

draft—The way NBA teams pick players each year.

forward—A player in the "frontcourt" who is counted on to rebound and score. Generally bigger than the guard.

free throws—Free shots given to a player after he is fouled. The shots are taken unguarded from the foul line.

guard—Usually the smallest player and best ball-handler on the court. Often the top scorers and top passers on the team.

NCAA—National Collegiate Athletic Association.

overtime—Extra time added on to a game that ends in a tie score.

playoffs—Games that decide the league champion when the regular season ends.

rebound—Grabbing the basketball after a missed shot.

three-point shot—A shot taken from beyond the three-point line. In high school and college, the line is nineteen feet nine inches from the basket. In the NBA, it is twenty-three feet nine inches away from the basket.

READING ABOUT

Books

McKissack, Fredrick. *Black Hoops: The History of African-Americans in Basketball*. New York: Scholastic, Inc., 1999.

Smith, Charles R. *Rimshots: Basketball Pix, Rolls and Rhythms*. New York: Penguin Putnam Books for Young Readers, 2000.

Yoder, Lou Gearhart. *A Ball, a Ball, a Basketball*. Warsaw, Ind.: LA Yoder, 2000.

Internet Addresses

The Official Web Site of the NBA
<http://www.nba.com/playerfile/glen_rice.html>

The Official Web Site of the Houston Rockets
<http://www.nba.com/rockets/>

INDEX

A

Anderson, Nick, 27

B

Big Ten, 18, 20
Bradley, Bill, 20
Bryant, Kobe, 38, 40

C

Chamberlain, Wilt, 36
Charlotte Hornets, 32, 34, 36
Chicago Bulls, 28, 30

F

Fisher, Steve, 22
Frieder, Bill, 18, 22

G

Golden State, 38
Gund Arena, 34

H

Houston Rockets, 5, 42

I

Indiana Pacers, 40

J

Jordan, Michael, 28, 30

L

Los Angeles Lakers, 38

M

Miami Heat, 7, 8, 10, 25, 27, 28,
    30, 32, 34
Michigan, University of, 7, 16,
    18, 20, 23
Morton, John, 22

N

National Basketball Association,
    5, 7, 8, 10, 12, 20, 23, 25, 28,
    30, 34, 36, 42
NBA All-Star Game, 34, 35, 36
NCAA, 20
New York Knicks, 42
Northwestern High School, 16

O

O'Neal, Shaquille, 38, 40
Orlando Magic, 8, 27, 30

P

Portland Trail Blazers, 40

R

Riley, Pat, 32
Robinson, Rumeal, 22

S

Seton Hall Pirates, 22

T

Toronto Raptors, 42